My ABC

Mein ABC

Bilingual Version
English / German

A list of the 26 letter Latin alphabet

in Arial and German handwriting (VA),
plus examples of other font styles

+ a short origin of letters
+ other language's letters sample
+ **cut cards for memorising**
+ **modern German handwriting
and old script tables**

euauthor@gmail.com

02.03.2014

This edition and version
direct publishing by
runaway penguins

ISBN-13: 978-1496062307
ISBN-10: 1496062302

Buy Print Version at the CreateSpace shop:
https://www.createspace.com/4688013

For questions and improvement
suggestions please contact:

euauthor@gmail.com

Fonts used: Arial, Verdana, etc. as distributed with MS Windows;
Suetterlin font © by R.G.Arens; VA Gruenewald font © by Peter
Wiegel, SIL Open fonts license 1.1; Pictures: all self drawn or
Wikipedia/GPL/public domain, book build from PNG Format (all
exported as curves/bitmaps, no embedded fonts)

Content

Latin Letters

A	B	C	D	E
F	G	H	I	J
K	L	M	N	O
P	Q	R	S	T
U	V	W	X	Y
		Z		

Ä, Ü, Ö will not be treated separately,
after all it is just two additional dots over the letter.

Plus a short introduction how to best approach
the letter learning business:
- The easy way to learn letters
- Frequency of occurrence of letters

The easy way to learn letters

Basically a child only needs to learn to read, write and spell one sentence and then theoretically can read, write and spell all letters of the alphabet (with a few exceptions, because certain letters spell differently in different combinations).

Examples of such a sentence to memorize the whole alphabet are shown below for different languages.

[GERMAN]

Franz jagt im komplett verwahrlosten Taxi quer durch Bayern.
oder
Zwölf Boxkämpfer jagen Viktor quer über
den großen Sylter Deich.

[ENGLISH]

The quick brown fox jumps over the lazy dog.
or
Jackdaws[1] love my big sphinx of quartz.

[FRENCH]

Portez ce whisky au vieux juge blond qui fume.

Yet, experience tells us that learning one sentence alone is not enough. Therefore this small booklet introduces the 26 letter Latin alphabet in different font styles and in most cases gives a short origin of those letters or examples of those letters in other languages' script. Additionally at the end of each letter's page a list of words that begin with the respective letter is given.

---

[1] a Jackdaw, is a passerine bird in the crow family.

Frequency of occurrence of letters in German and English texts

Having watched the German version of "Wheel of Fortune" one becomes aware that it is beneficial to winning the game if one knows the frequency of occurrence of letters in German texts.

The following table shows the rank of occurrence of letters in German and English texts (Umlaute treated as their basic letter).

[GERMAN]				[ENGLISH]			
Rank	Letter	Rank	Letter	Rank	Letter	Rank	Letter
1	E	14	L	1	E	14	M
2	N	15	B	2	T	15	W
3	I	16	O	3	A	16	F
4	S	17	F	4	O	17	G
5	T	18	K	5	I	18	Y
6	R	19	W	6	N	19	P
7	A	20	V	7	S	20	B
8	D	21	Z	8	H	21	V
9	H	22	P	9	R	22	K
10	U	23	J	10	D	23	J
11	G	24	Q	11	L	24	X
12	M	25	Y	12	C	25	Q
13	C	26	X	13	U	26	Z

Source: Fletcher Pratt, Secret and Urgent: the Story of Codes and Ciphers, Blue Ribbon Books, 1939, pp. 256-257. and Robert Edward Lewand, Cryptographical Mathematics, The Mathematical Association of America, 2000

The list of the 26 letter alphabet is arranged in its standard order from "A to Z". If teachers and parents would like introduce the letters according to their actual frequency of occurrence (i.e. their importance, "Seba's ETINA method ®") they will find the letter ranks for both the German, English and the combined ranks in the top right corner of each page.

[Combined Rank English and German]

Rank	2	7	8	8	10	11	15	17	18	20	23	25	25
Letter	E	T	I	N	A	S	R	H	D	O	U	C	L

Rank	26	28	33	34	35	40	41	41	43	46	47	49	50
Letter	M	G	F	W	B	K	P	V	Y	J	Z	Q	X

Alphabet pages + cards

The following alphabet pages can be cut in half thereby letting you prepare cards with the letter in Arial font and the example words, for learning by cards ... leaving the other half with the letter's pronunciation (English/German) and its origin in the book for reference.

This e-book was build from PNG pictures using Amazons Comic Book Creator. A print version of this Book can be ordered over Amazon Create Space or similar POD service. However Amazon Create Space does not support printing in the portrait format and binding at the shortest side. Cutting out the ABC cards is a little more cumbersome with the POD Version (I do hope that issue gets addressed in the future.

Future editions of this book might include:

- mnemonic phrases and pictures for each letter page to support learning
- additional pages for learning numbers (1-10)
- writing exercise pages for letters, most common bigrams and trigrams in both languages
- a list with most common and short words for both languages (for exercise)
- a glossary with free study resources on the web

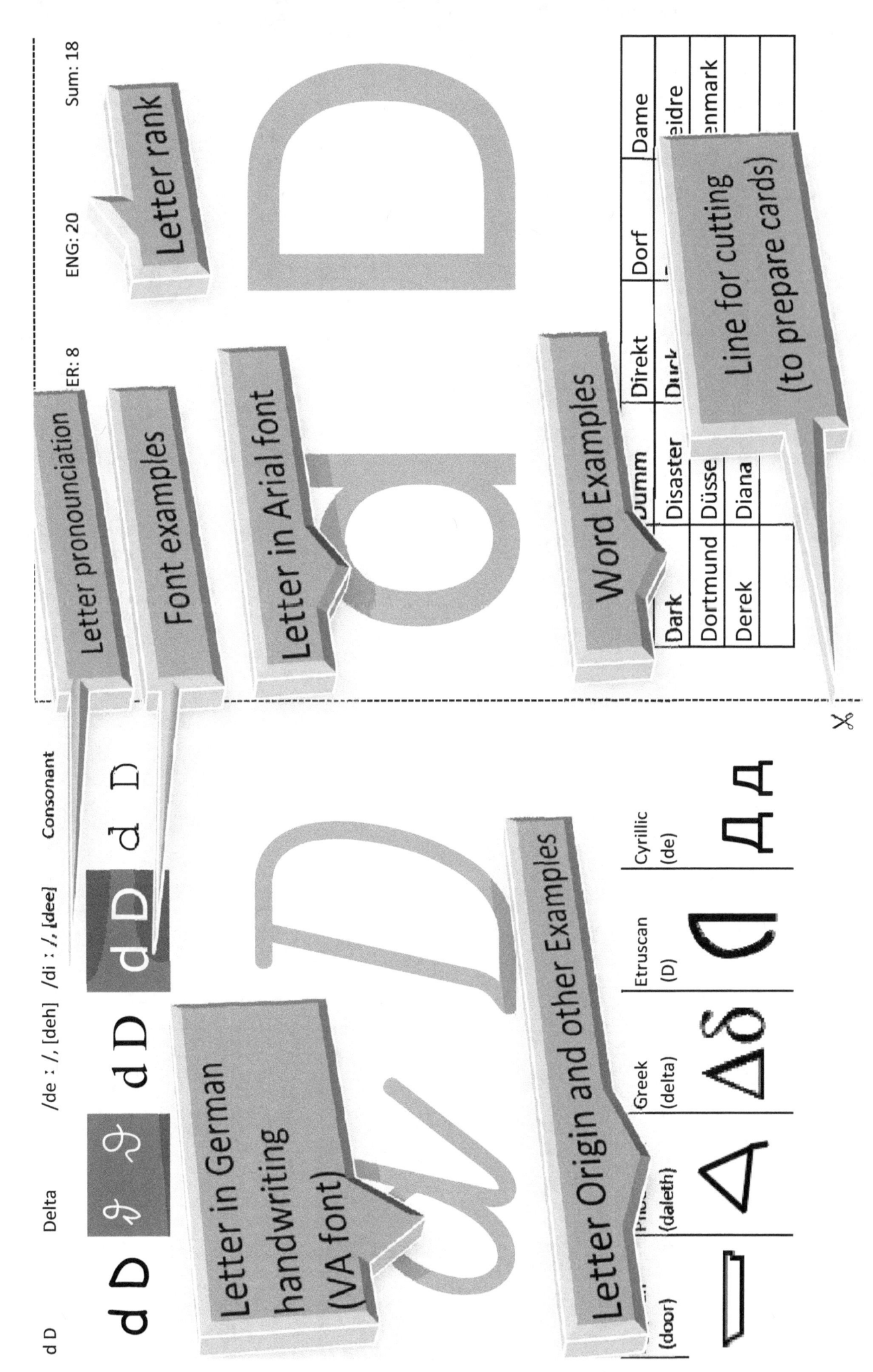

d D   Delta   /de : /, [deh]   /di : /, [dee]   Consonant

ER: 8   ENG: 20   Sum: 18

Letter pronounciation

Font examples

Letter rank

Letter in Arial font

Letter in German handwriting (VA font)

Letter Origin and other Examples

(door)	Phoen (daleth)	Greek (delta)	Etruscan (D)	Cyrillic (de)

Word Examples

Dark	Direkt	Dorf	Dame
Dortmund	Disaster	Durk	Deidre
Derek	Düsse	Diana	Denmark

Line for cutting (to prepare cards)

a A Alfa /aː/, [ah] /eɪ/, [eyh] Vokal / Vowel

GER: 7 ENG: 3 Sum: 10

a A   ɑ A   a A   a A

A

a

Apfel	Auto	Abfall	Abend	Ast
Apple	Automatic	Action	Actual	And
Alpha	America	Argentinia	Angola	Austria
Anna	Andre	Anton		

A α

Egyptian	Phoenician (aleph)	Greek (Alpha)	Etruscan (A)	Roman/Cyrillic (A)

b B

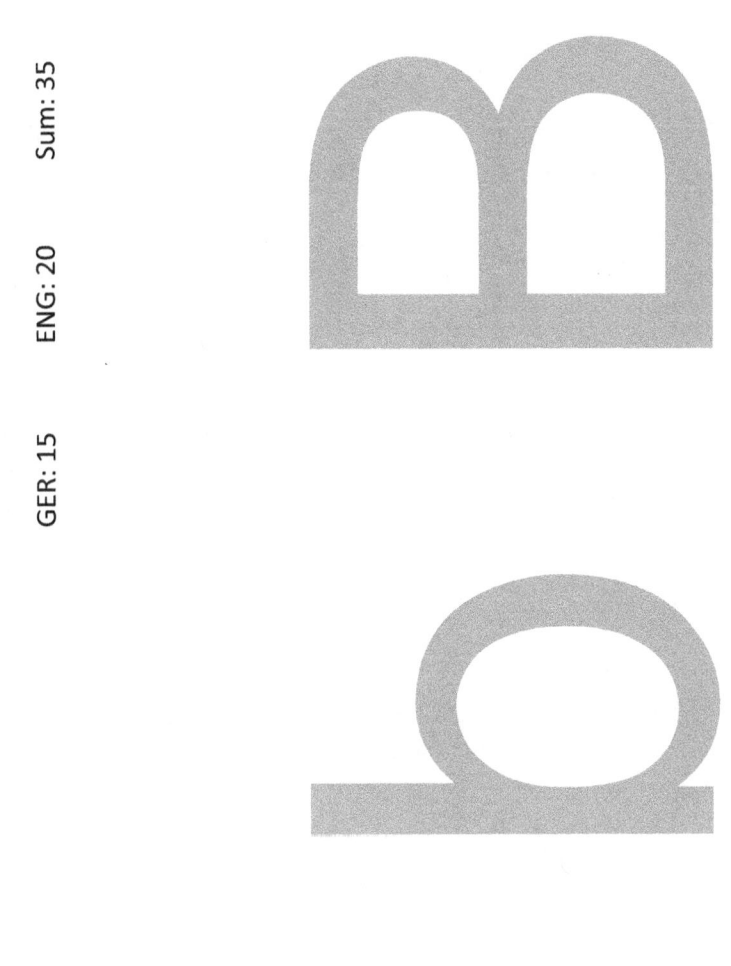

Bier	Bär	Bunt	Bald	Bieber
Big	Baby	Berlin	Beta	Bravo
Brazil	Bhutan	Bulgaria	Belgium	Belize
Bernd	Babette	Bahrain		

---

b B

Bravo　　　/be : / [beh]　　/bi : / [bee]　　Consonant

b B　　b B　　b　B

Egyptian (cottage)	Phoenician (beth)	Greek (Beta)	Etruscan (B)	Cyrillic (Be)
	⅁	Β β	𐌁	Б б

c C   Charlie   GER: 13   ENG: 12   Sum: 25

Charlie   /ʧe : / [zeh]   /si : / [cee]   Consonant

c C   c C   c C   C C

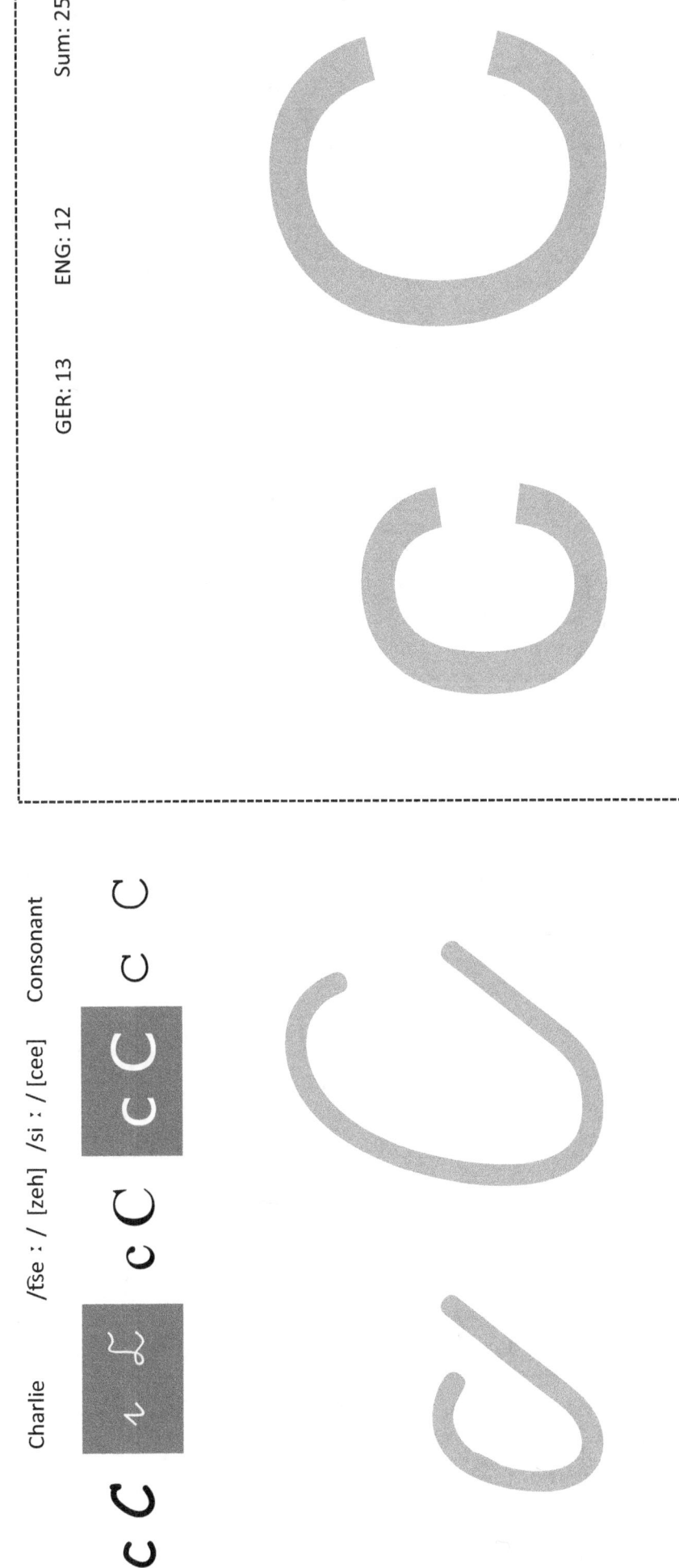

Charakter	Charm	China	Cicero	Castor
Charisma	Caesar	Chef	Chimp	Charles
Cambodia	Chile	Canada	Chad	Colombia
Carter	Cecillie	Cyprus		

Phoenician (gaml)	Arabic (ǧīm)	Hebrew (gimel)	Greek (gamma)	Etruscan (C)
𐤂	ﺝ	ג	Γ γ	⊃

d D Delta /deː/, [deh] /diː/, [dee] Consonant GER: 8 ENG: 10 Sum: 18

d D d D d D

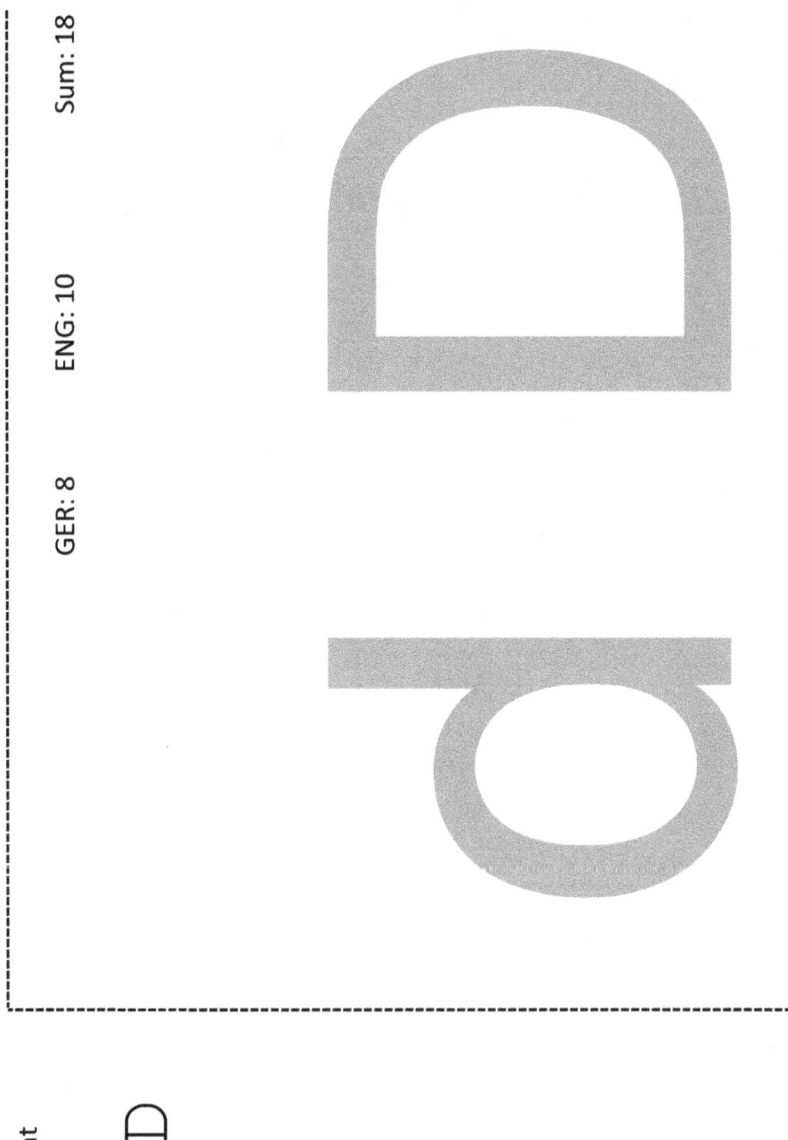

Deutsch	Dumm	Direkt	Dorf	Dame
Dark	Disaster	Duck	Dune	Deidre
Dortmund	Düsseldorf	Dallas	Daytona	Denmark
Derek	Diana	Dominica		

Egyptian (door)	Phoenician (daleth)	Greek (delta)	Etruscan (D)	Cyrillic (de)
	△ △	Δ δ	⟨ ◖	Д д

e E Echo /ʔe : /, [eh] /i : / [eeh] Vokal / Vowel

GER: 1 ENG: 1 Sum: 2

e E e E e E

Ese	Einfach	Eimer	Ei	Eis
Efficient	East	Energy	Earth	Ear
Election	Essen	Ecuador	Ethiopia	Estonia
Emma	Erik	Egypt		

Egyptian (q')	Phoenician (daleth)	Etruscan (e)	Greek (epsilon)	Japanese (e)

f F   Delta   /ɛf/, [ef]   /ɛf/, [ef]   Consonant

GER: 17   ENG: 16   Sum: 33

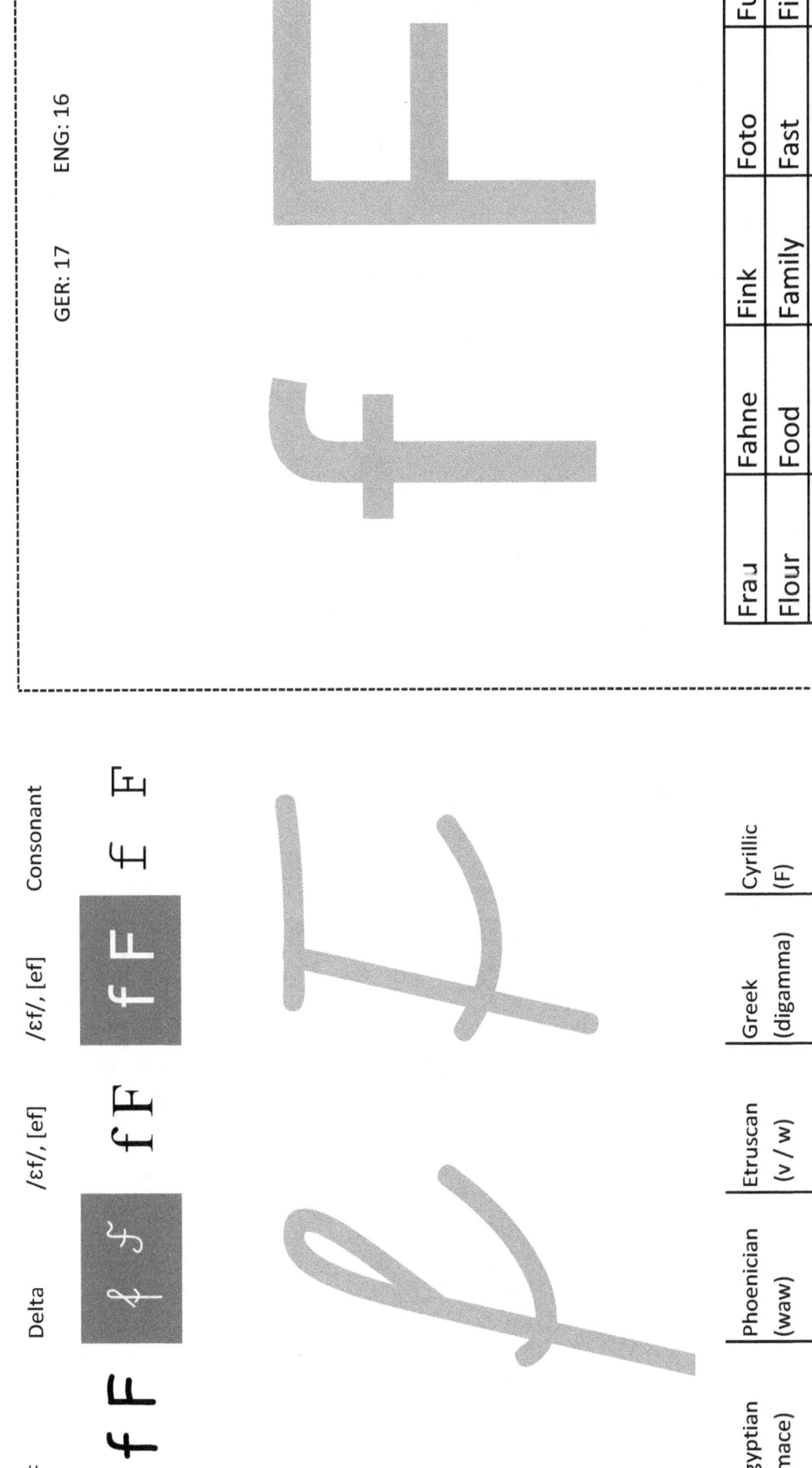

Frau	Fahne	Fink	Foto	Futter
Flour	Food	Family	Fast	File
Federation	Fiji	Finland	France	Egypt
Flora	Florian	Florida		

Egyptian (mace)	Phoenician (waw)	Etruscan (v / w)	Greek (digamma)	Cyrillic (F)

g G   Golf   /geː/, [geh]   /dʒiː/ [gee]   Consonant

g G   g G

GER: 11   ENG: 17   Sum: 28

Gehen	Gabel	Gern	Garten	Gast
Galaxy	Gold	German	Go	Good
Gambia	Germany	Ghana	Greece	Guam
Gunther	Gabriella	Garfield		

Latin (gamma)	Latin (yogh)	Greek (gamma)	Cyrillic (Ge)
Ɣ	Ʒ	Γ	Г
ɣ	ʒ	γ	г

h H Delta /ha ː /, [ha] /eɪtʃ/, [aitch] Consonant

GER: 9 ENG: 8 Sum: 17

h H h H h H

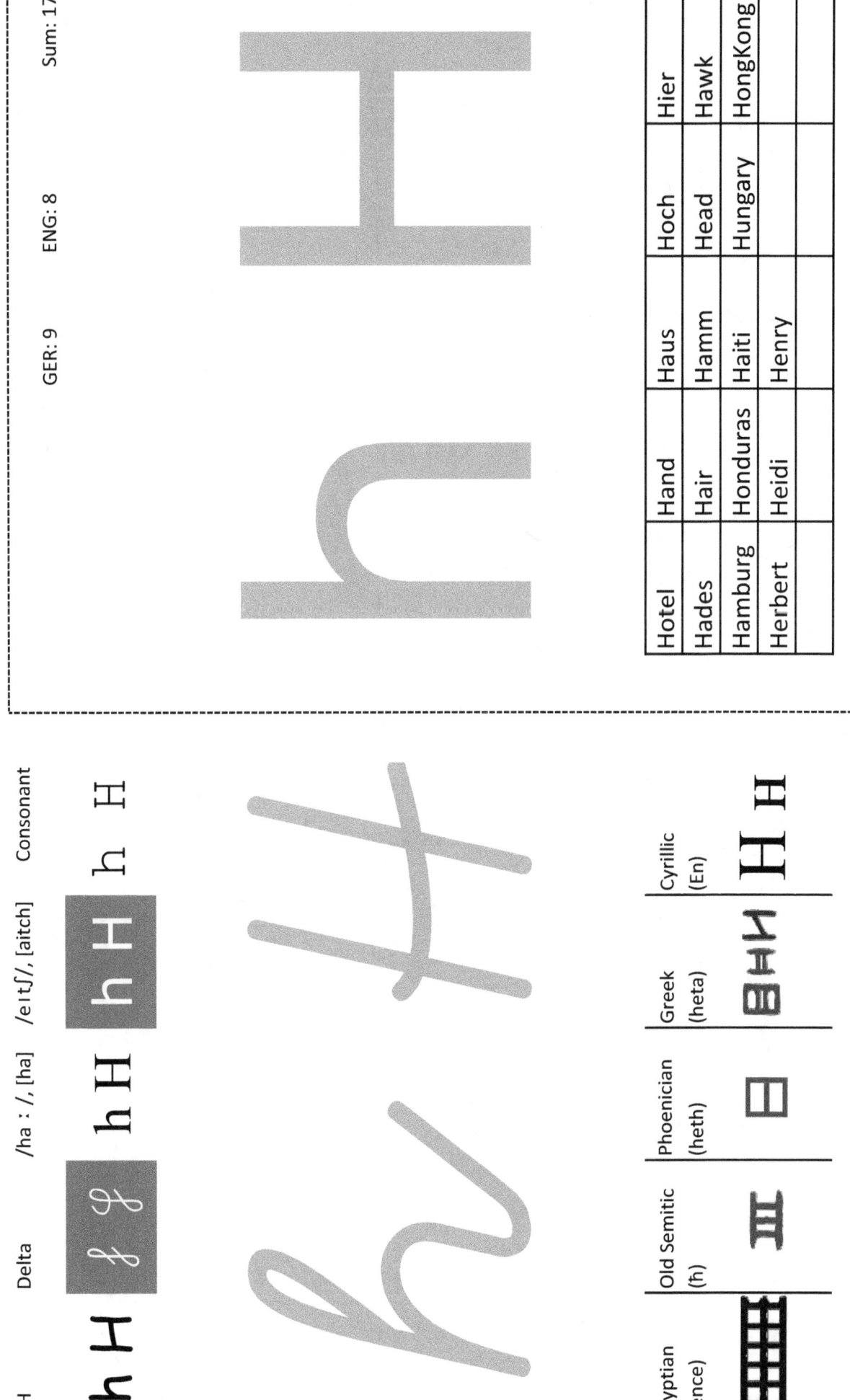

	Hotel	Hand	Haus	Hoch	Hier
	Hades	Hair	Hamm	Head	Hawk
	Hamburg	Honduras	Haiti	Hungary	HongKong
	Herbert	Heidi	Henry		

Egyptian (fence)	Old Semitic (h)	Phoenician (heth)	Greek (heta)	Cyrillic (En)

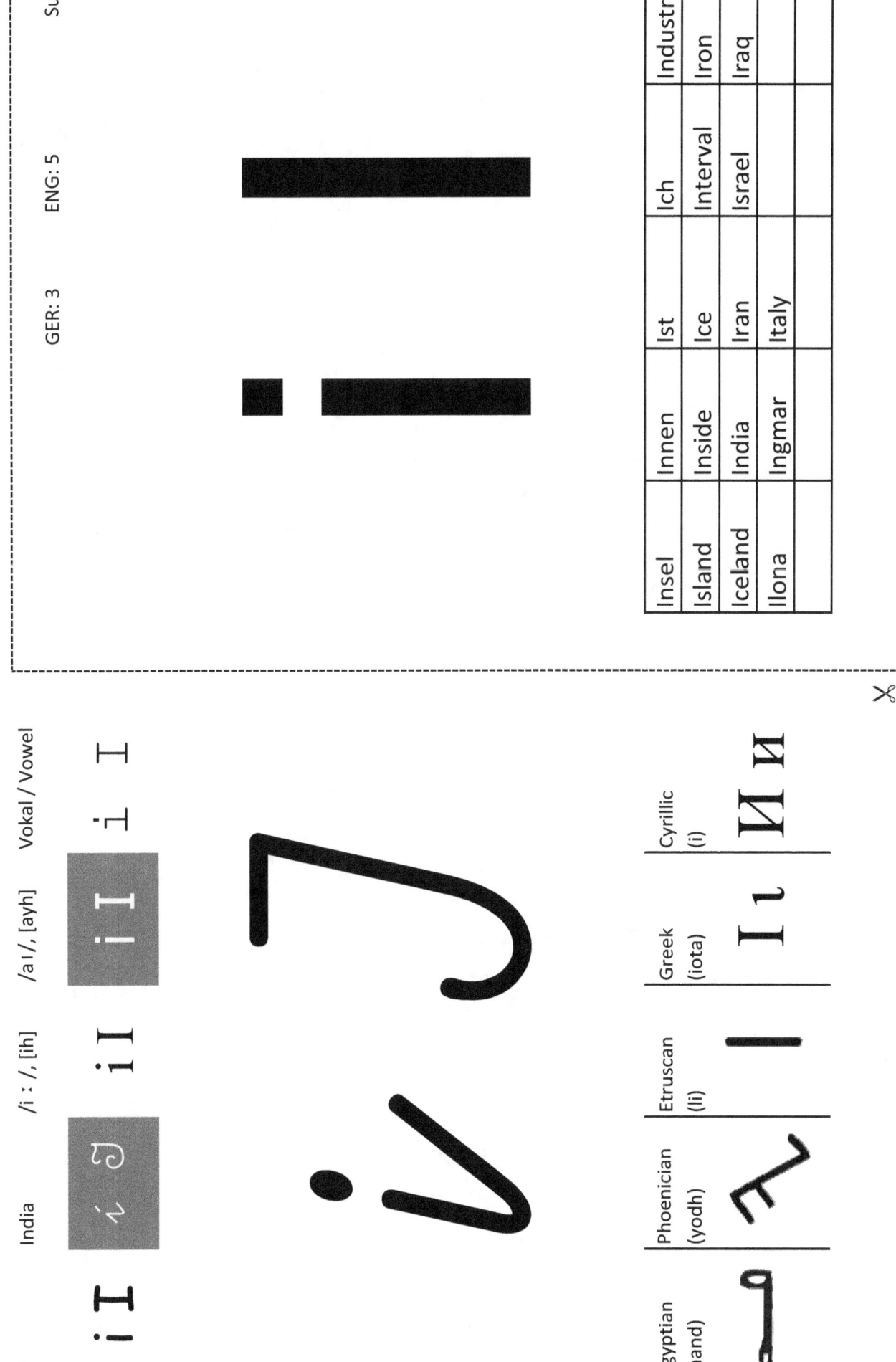

i I

India /i ː /, [ih] /aɪ/, [ayh] Vokal / Vowel

i ì iI   iI   i ì I   I

GER: 3   ENG: 5   Sum: 8

Insel	Innen	Ist	Ich	Industrie
Island	Inside	Ice	Interval	Iron
Iceland	India	Iran	Israel	Iraq
Ilona	Ingmar	Italy		

Egyptian (hand)	Phoenician (yodh)	Etruscan (Ii)	Greek (iota)	Cyrillic (i)
			Ι ι	И И

j J   Juliet   /jɔt/, [jot]   /dʒeɪ/, [jay]   Consonant

j ȷ ȷ ȷ   j J   j J   j J

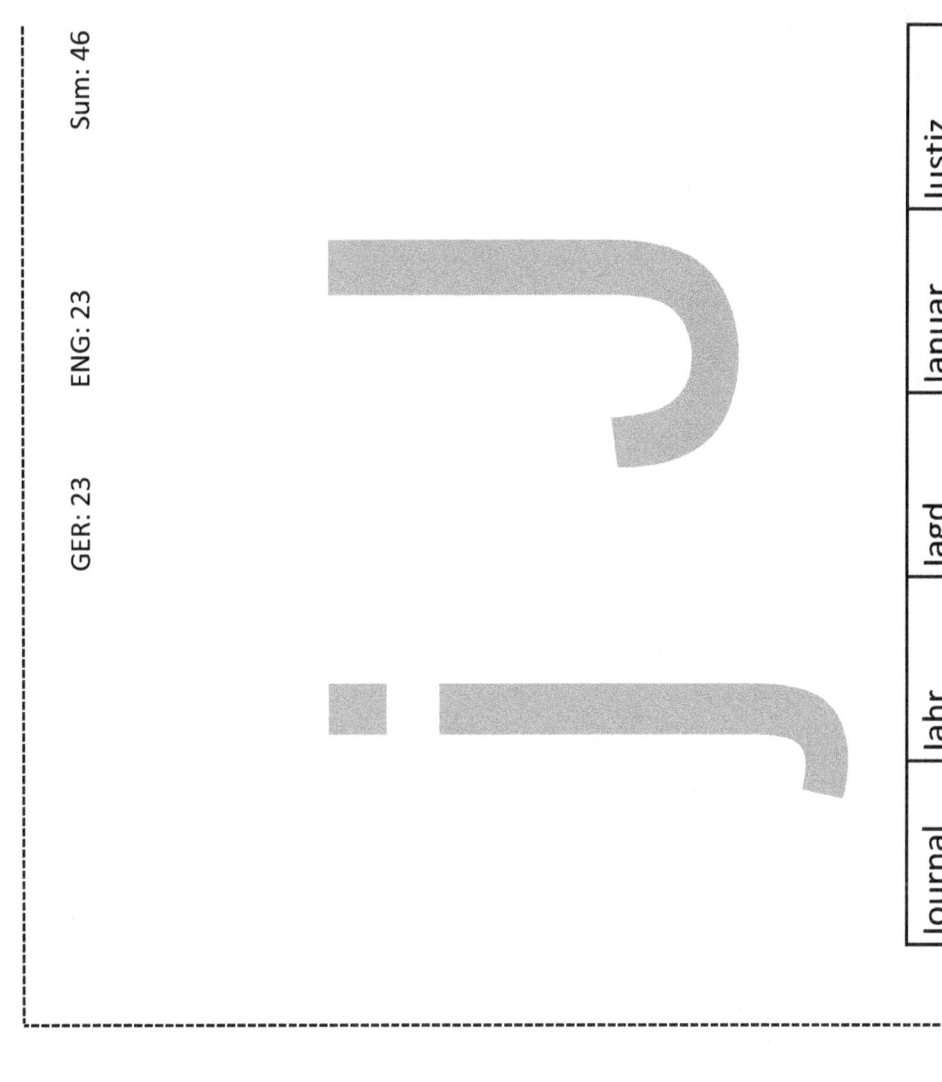

(origin: split from "i" quite recently,

originally, 'I' and 'J' were different shapes for the same letter)

GER: 23   ENG: 23   Sum: 46

Journal	Jahr	Jagd	Januar	Justiz
Jacket	Jeans	Jewellery	Jelly	Job
Jamaica	Japan	Jordan	Justitian	Justice
Julia	Jakob	Jerry		

k K   Kilo   /kʰaː/, [kah] /keɪ//, [kay]   Consonant

GER: 18   ENG: 22   Sum: 40

k K   k K   k K

Karte	Kaufen	Kind	Karneval	Kampf
Knee	Kiss	Knight	Kitchen	King
Kenya	Kuwait	Kazakhst.	Keiko	Kaspar
Karl	Kathrina	Kassandra		

Egyptian (hand, D)	Proto-Semitic (K)	Phoenician (kaph)	Etruscan (K)	Greek (Kappa)
		⪫	K	Κ κ

GER: 14   ENG: 11   Sum: 25

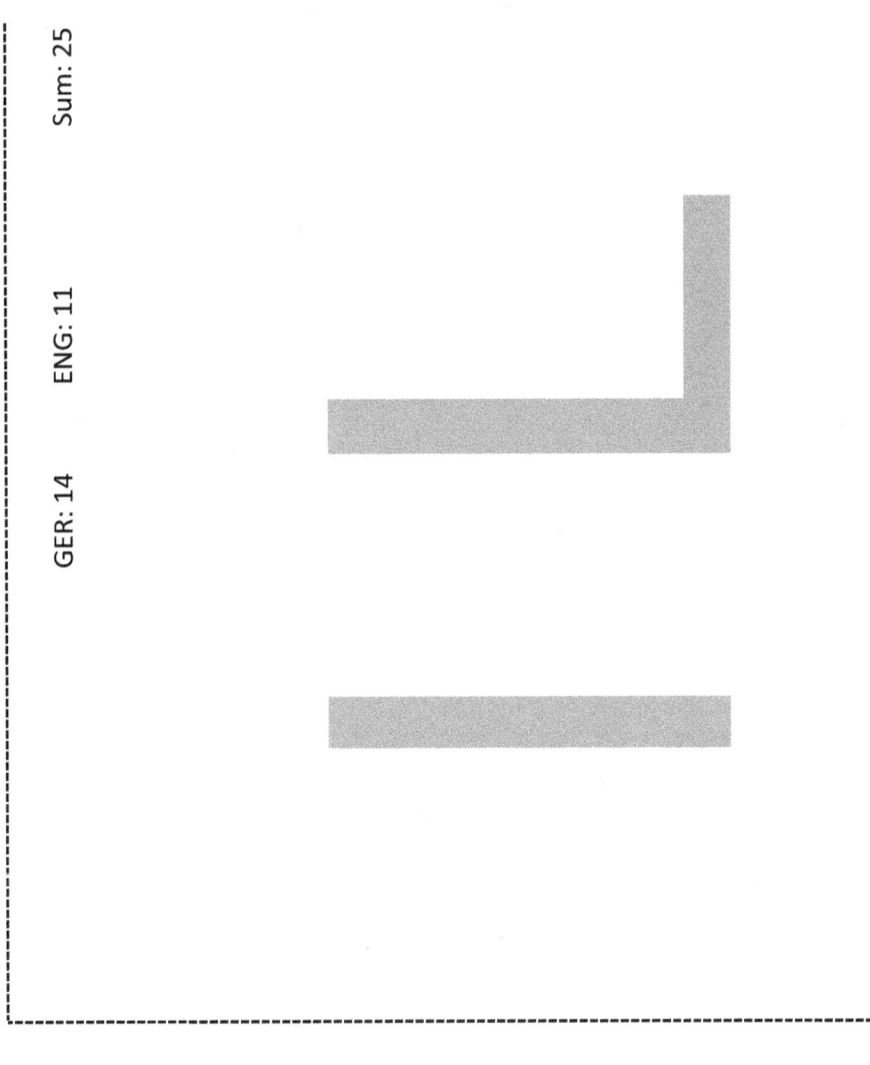

Liebe	Laufen	Land	Lob	Leben
Life	Love	Listen	Lamb	Lady
Lacs	Liberia	Latvia	Lybia	Lithuania
Lara	Lancelot	Lebanon		

Egyptian (staff, prod)	Phoenician (lamedh)	Etruscan (L)	Greek (lambda)	Cyrillic (El)

m M   Mike   /ɛm/, [em]   /ɛm/, [em]   Consonant

m M m M m M m M

m M m m M

Egyptian (water, N)	Phoenician (mem)	Etruscan (M)	Greek (Mu)	Cyrillic (Em)
			M μ	M m

✂

GER: 12   ENG: 14   Sum: 26

m M

Mama	Maus	Meister	Mangan	Mais
Metal	Machine	Mail	Mass	Meadow
Mali	Malaysia	Morocco	Mexico	Mongolia
Maria	Manfred	Myanmar		

n N November /ɛn/, [en] /ɛn/, [en] Consonant

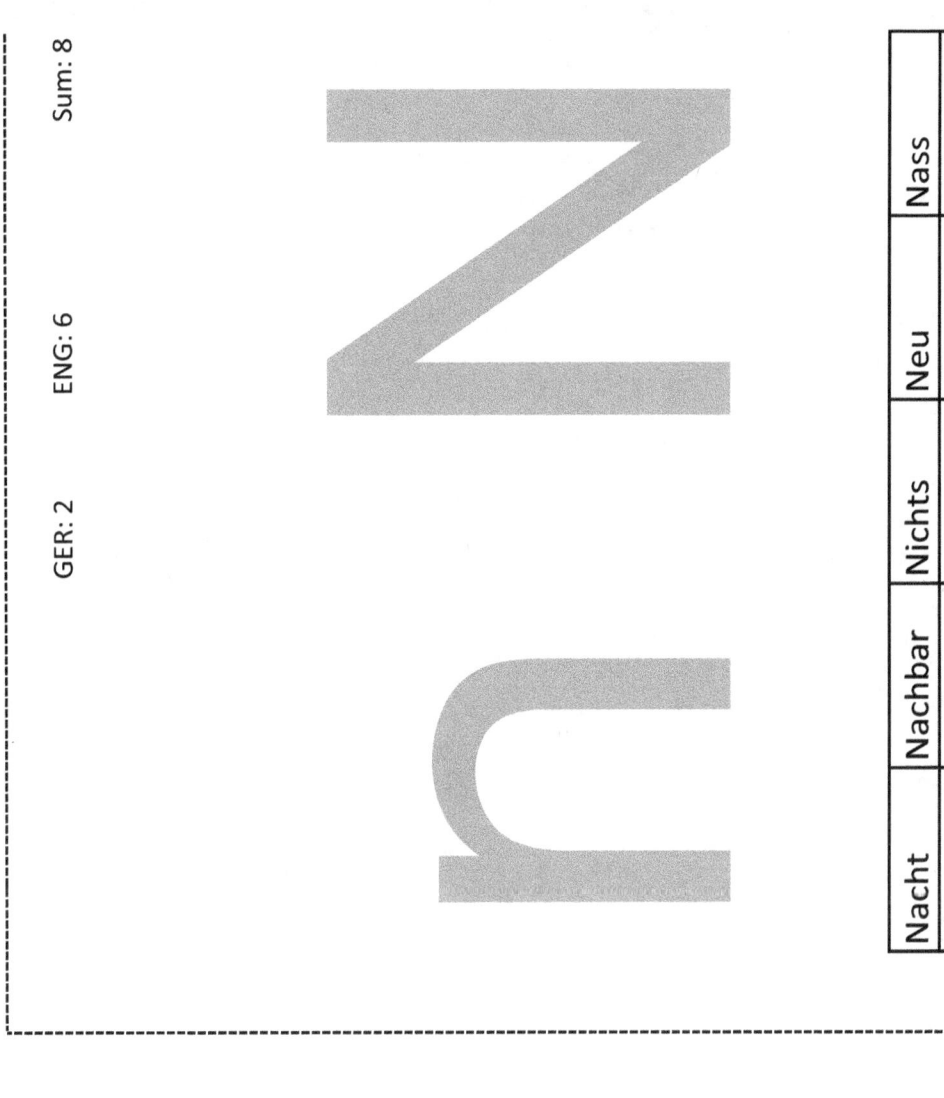

	Nacht	Nachbar	Nichts	Neu	Nass
	New	Nothing	Near	North	Name
	Nepal	Norway	Nicaragua	Niger	Nigeria
	Nira	Norbert	Namibia		

GER: 2 ENG: 6 Sum: 8

	Egyptian (snake)	Phoenician (N)	Etruscan (N)	Greek (Nu)	Cyrillic (i)
		𐤍	𐌍	Ν ν	И и

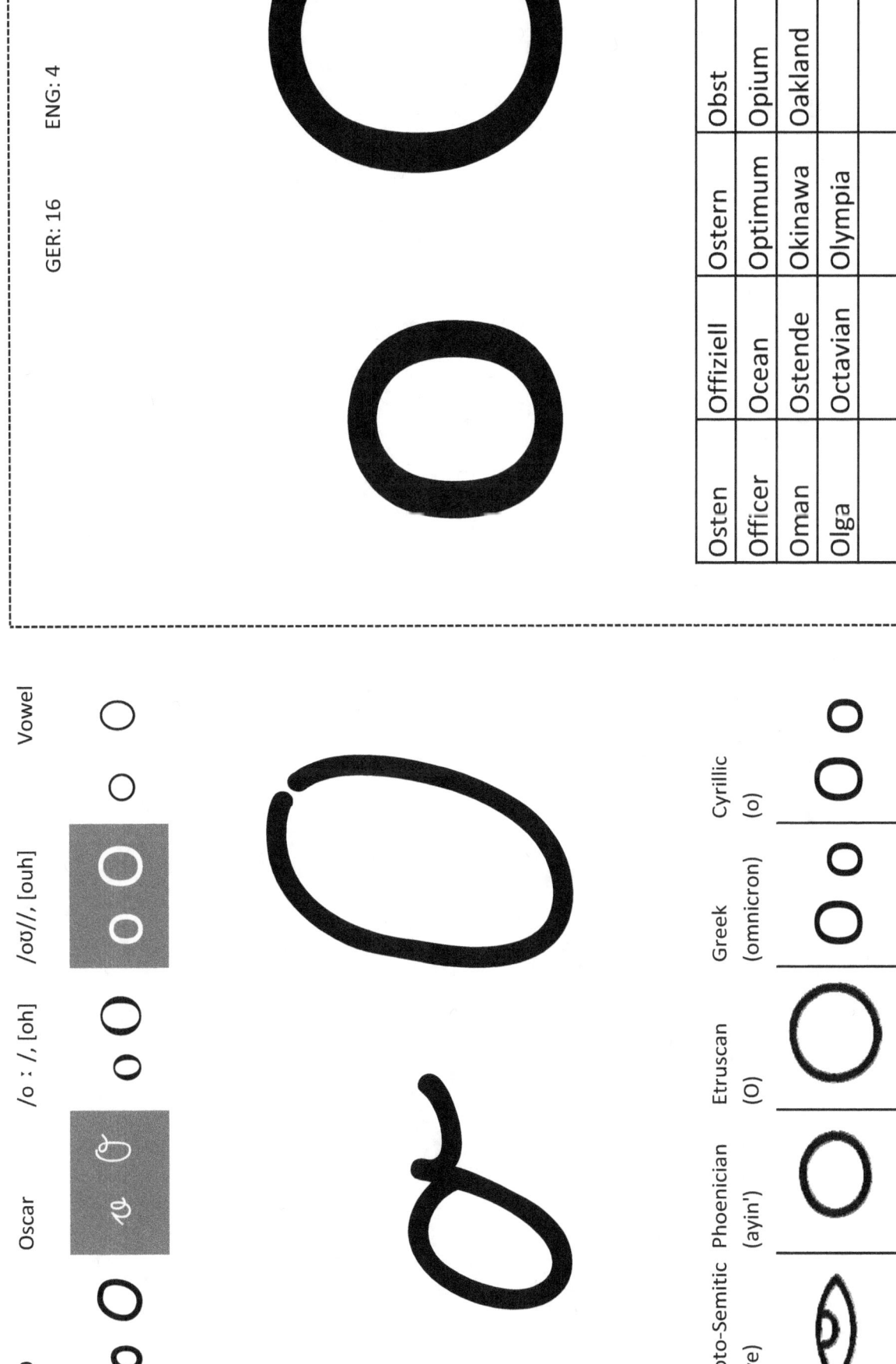

o O   Oscar   /oː/, [oh]   /oʊ//, [ouh]   Vowel

GER: 16   ENG: 4   Sum: 20

Osten	Offiziell	Ostern	Obst	Ochse
Officer	Ocean	Optimum	Opium	Onion
Oman	Ostende	Okinawa	Oakland	Oliver
Olga	Octavian	Olympia		

Proto-Semitic (eye)   Phoenician (ayin')   Etruscan (O)   Greek (omnicron)   Cyrillic (o)

p P Papa /pʰe/, [peh] /pi:/, [pee] Consonant

GER: 22   ENG: 19   Sum: 41

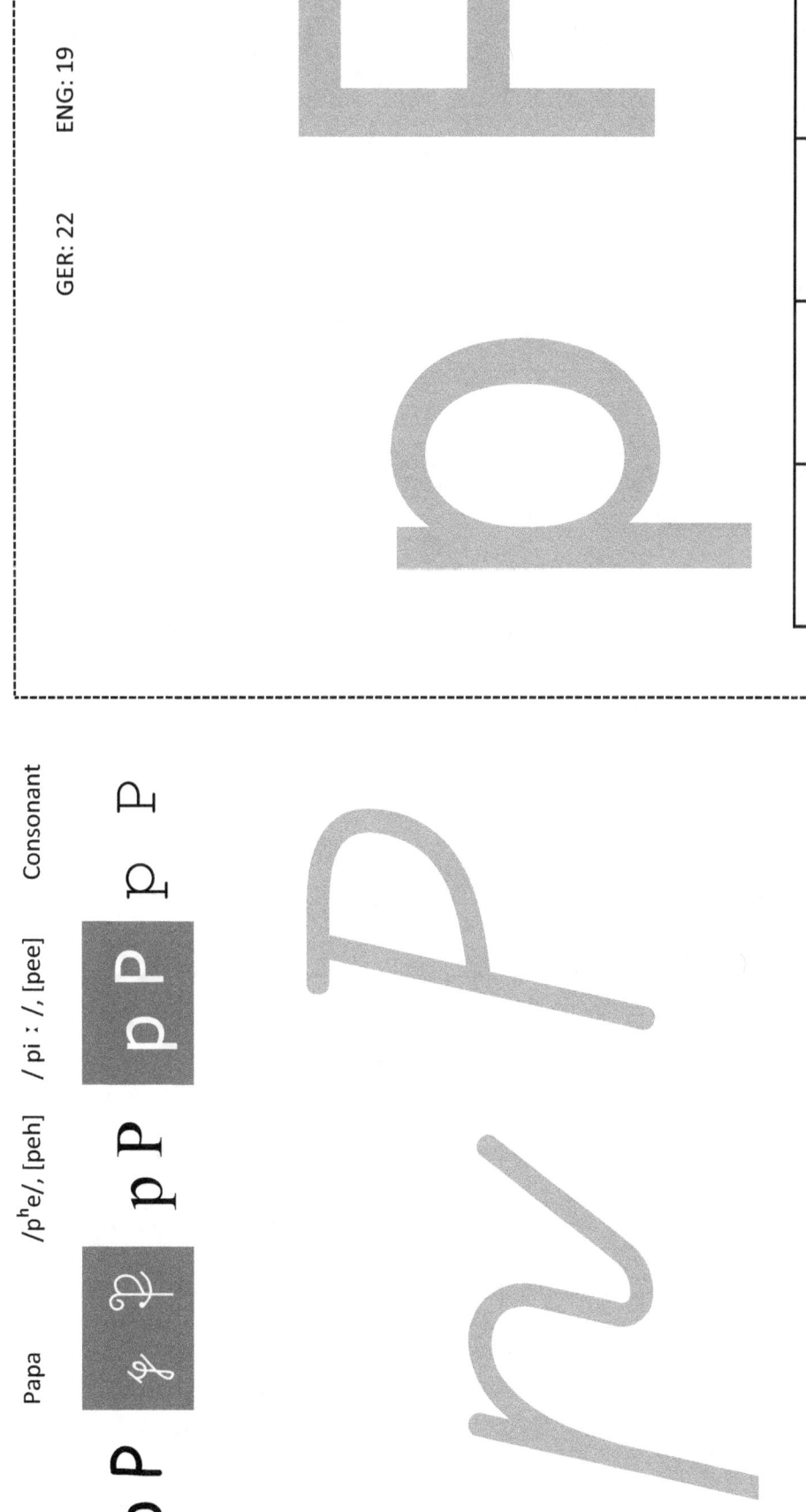

Post	Porto	Pause	Pfirsich	Pflaume
Peer	Picture	Parcel	Pain	Peace
Peru	Poland	Portugal	Portland	Phillipines
Petra	Peter	Pakistan		

Proto-Semitic (thowing stick) (Pe)	Phoenician (Pe)	Etruscan (P)	Greek (pi)	Hebrew (p)
		ๅ	Π π	฿ ๆ

q Q   Quebec   /kʰu/, [kuh]   /kju/, [cue]   Consonant

GER: 24   ENG: 25   Sum: 49

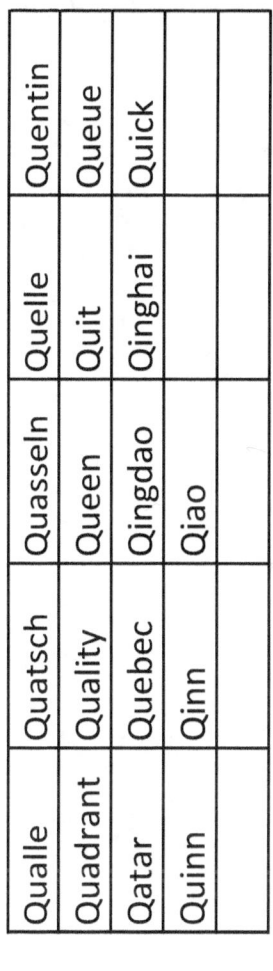

Qualle	Quatsch	Quasseln	Quelle	Quentin
Quadrant	Quality	Queen	Quit	Queue
Qatar	Quebec	Qingdao	Qinghai	Quick
Quinn	Qinn	Qiao		

Egyptian (cord of wool)	Phoenician (qoph)	Etruscan (Q)	Greek (qoppa)	Cyrillic (kje)

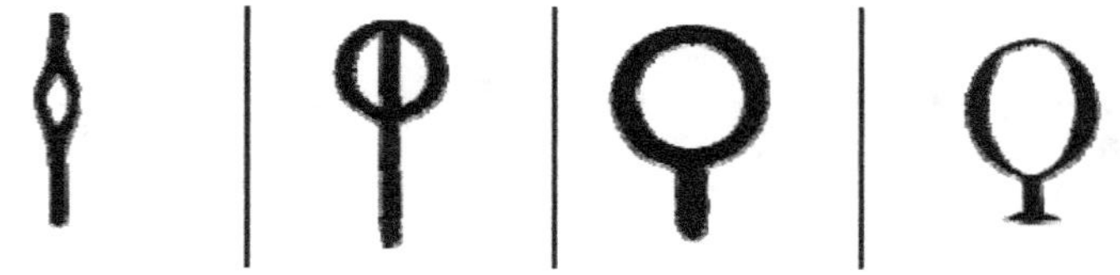

r R Romeo /r/, [er] /ɑr/, [ar] Consonant

r R

ℛ r R ɾ R

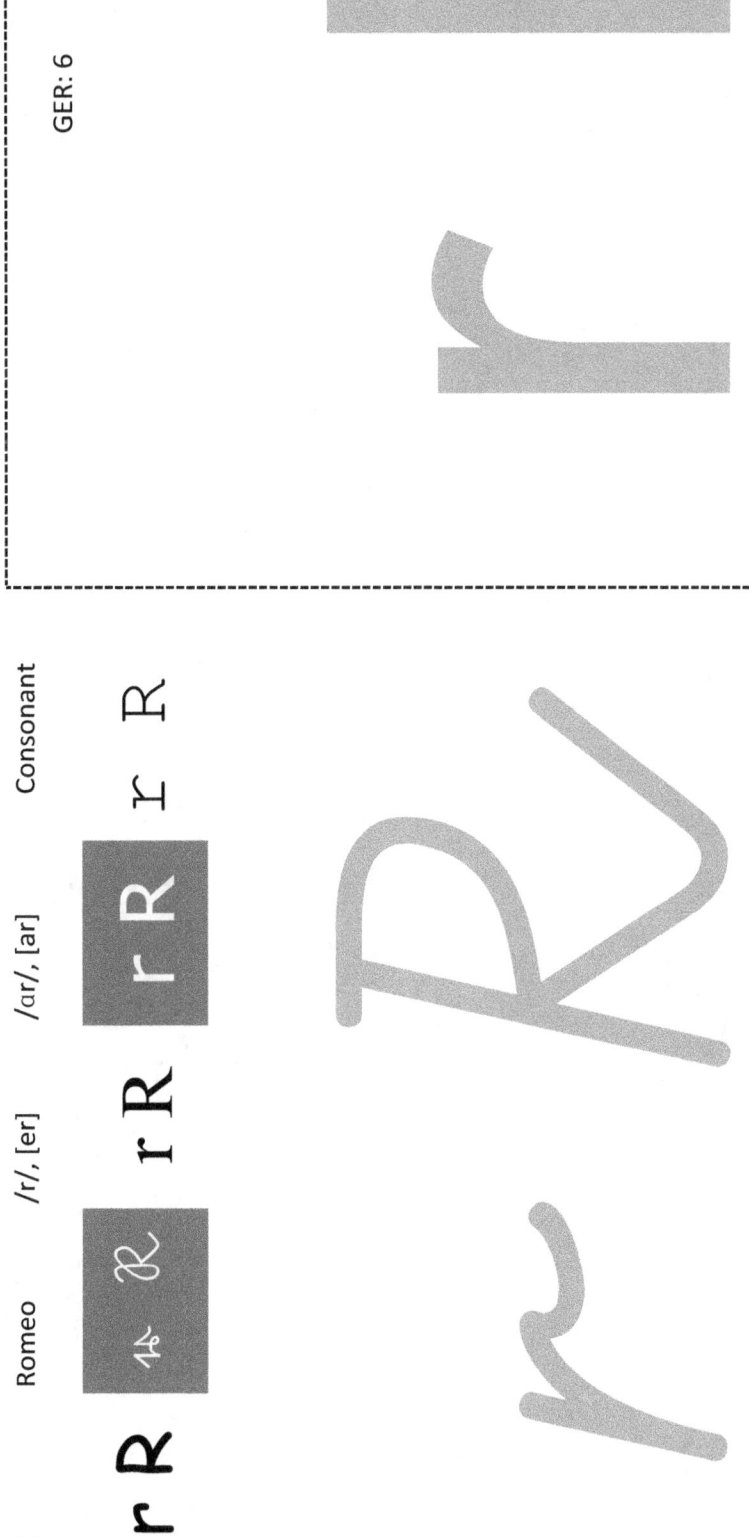

r R GER: 6 ENG: 9 Sum: 15

Räuber	Rand	Rose	Richtig	Rad
Road	Rabbit	Radio	Red	Right
Reunion	Romania	Russia	Rwanda	Republic
Rita	Richter	Roland		

Egyptian (head, tp)	Phoenician (resh)	Etruscan (R)	Greek (rho)	Cyrillic (Ya)
	◁ 4 9	4 4	Ρ ρ	Я я

s S   Sierra   /ɛs/, [es]   /ɛs/, [ess]   Consonant

GER: 4   ENG: 7   Sum: 11

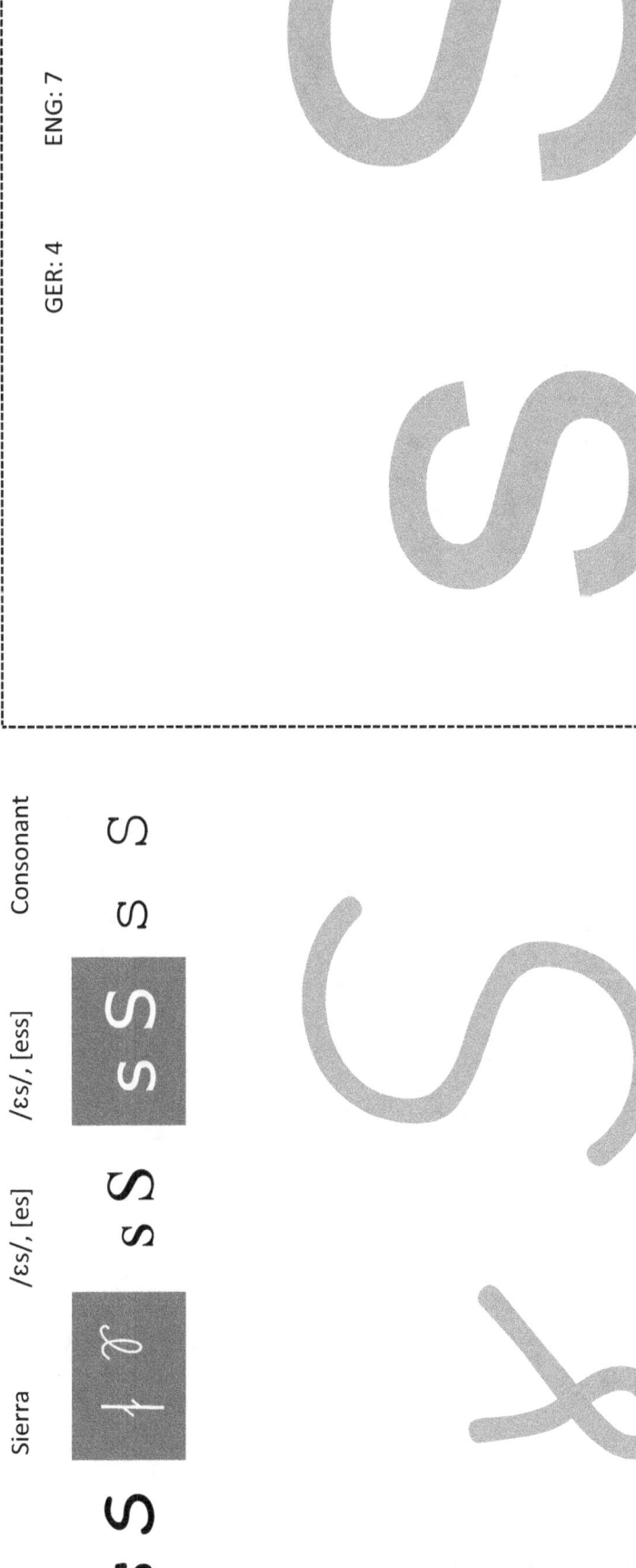

See	Sachen	Saft	Süden	Seife
South	Special	Secure	Saturday	Scale
Serbia	Singapore	Slovakia	Syria	Sweden
Sabrina	Simon	Sudan		

Proto-Semitic (Bow)	Phoenician (shin)	Etruscan (S)	Greek (sigma)	Cyrillic (Es)
Ϻ	W	Ϟ	Σ σ ς	С с

t T

Tango /tʰeː]/, [teh] /tiː/, [tee] Consonant

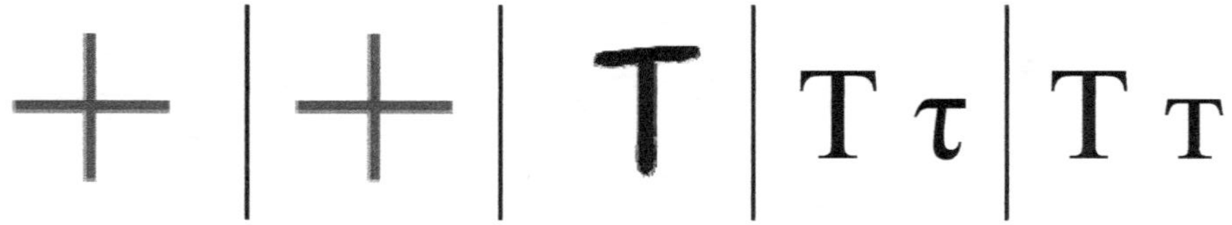

GER: 5 ENG: 2 Sum: 7

t T

Tür	Tod	Tag	Telefon	Taube
Today	Table	Tooth	Tea	Time
Taiwan	Trinidad	Tuvalu	Tibet	Togo
Tani	Teresa	Thomas		

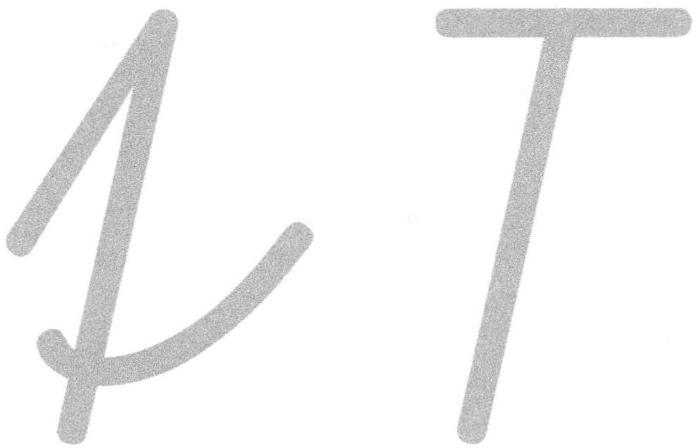

Proto-Semitic (a cross)	Phoenician (taw)	Etruscan (T)	Greek (tau)	Cyrillic (Te)
		T	Τ τ	Т Т

u U   Uniform   /u :]/, [uh]   /ju : /, [you]   Vokal / Vowel

GER: 10   ENG: 13   Sum: 23

Umwelt	Uhrzeit	Unfall	Ur-Oma	Ursprung
Umbrella	Urban	Untidy	Ultimatum	Utility
Uganda	Ukraine	Uruguay	Uzbekist.	United ..
Ursula	Unger	Ulysses		

Proto-Semitic (waw)	Phoenician (waw)	Etruscan (V)	Greek (ypsilon)	Japanese (u)
ϙ	Y	Υ	Υ	う
ϙ	Y	Y	Υ	い
			υ	え

v V Victor /faʊ/, [Fau] / vi : /, [vee] Consonant

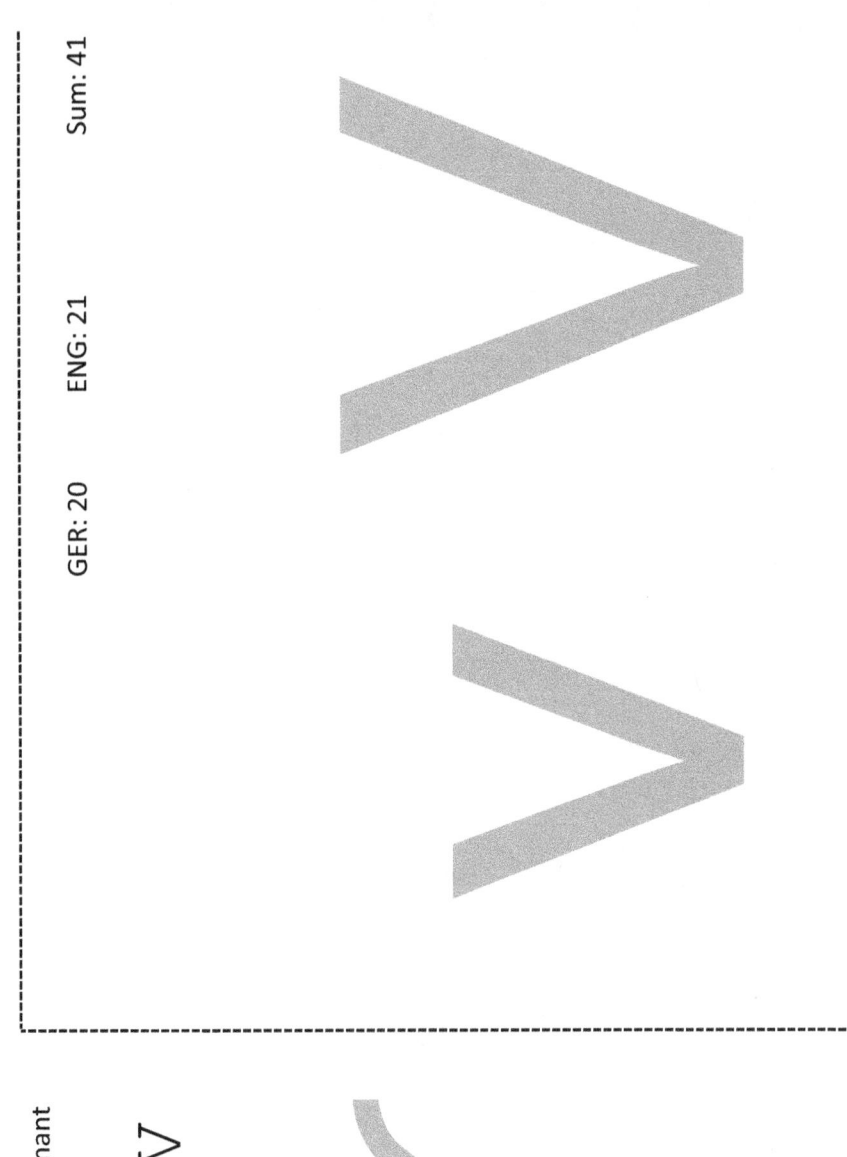

Sum: 41

GER: 20 ENG: 21

Vater	Vanillie	Ventil	Verein	Verletzung
Vaccum	Vaccine	Verb	Village	Voice
Vancouver	Venezuala	Vietnam	Vega	Venice
Valdemar	Vanessa	Valencia		

(origin: same as "U")

✂

w W Whiskey /veː/, [weh] /w/, double-u Consonant

w W

W W W w

w m ω W

(same Origin as "u" and "v"
derived from a double "u")

GER: 19   ENG: 15   Sum: 34

Wolle	Wasser	Warm	Winter	Wind
West	Wheat	Waffle	Web	Walk
Wallis	Whitehall	Waterloo	Wharton	Windsor
Wendy	William	Willow		

x X X-ray /ɪks/, [iks] /ɛks/, [ex] Consonant

GER: 26   ENG: 24   Sum: 50

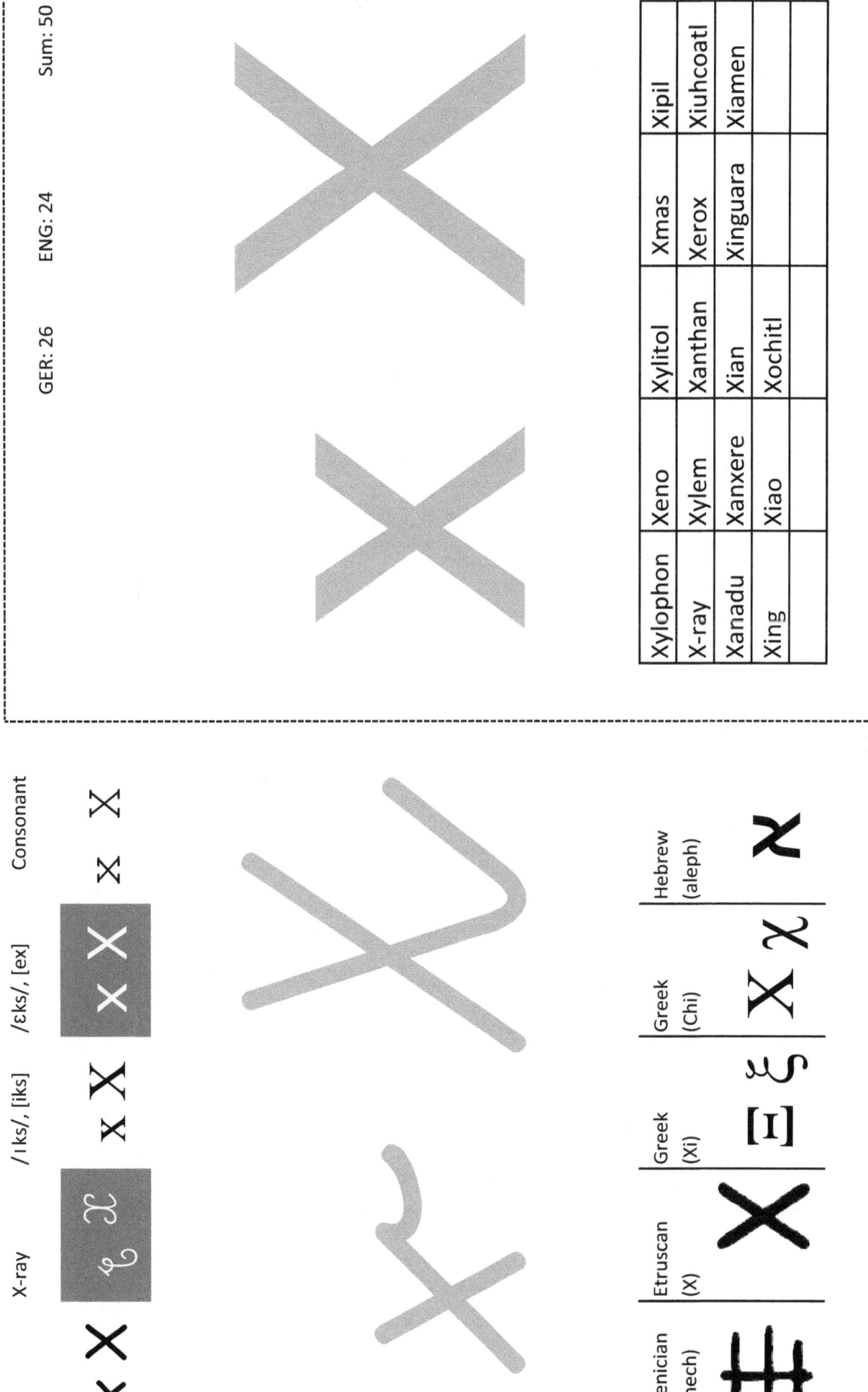

Xylophon	Xeno	Xylitol	Xmas	Xipil
X-ray	Xylem	Xanthan	Xerox	Xiuhcoatl
Xanadu	Xanxere	Xian	Xinguara	Xiamen
Xing	Xiao	Xochitl		

| Phoenician (samech) | Etruscan (X) | Greek (Xi) | Greek (Chi) | Hebrew (aleph) |

y Y Yankee /ih/, Ypsilon /waɪ/, [wye] Consonant/Vowel GER: 25 ENG: 18 Sum: 34

Yoga	Yoghurt	Ventil	Yin	Yang
Yacht	Yard	Yellow	Yield	Yuen
Yemen	Yale	York	Yuki	Yakov
Yani	Yuki	Yoshi		

(same origin as "U" and "V")

z Z | Zulu | /tsɛt]/, [tzet] | /zɛd/ /, [zed] | Consonant

z Z z Z z Z z Z z Z

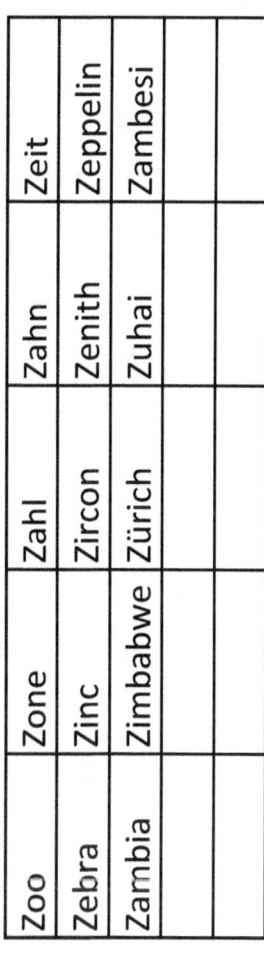

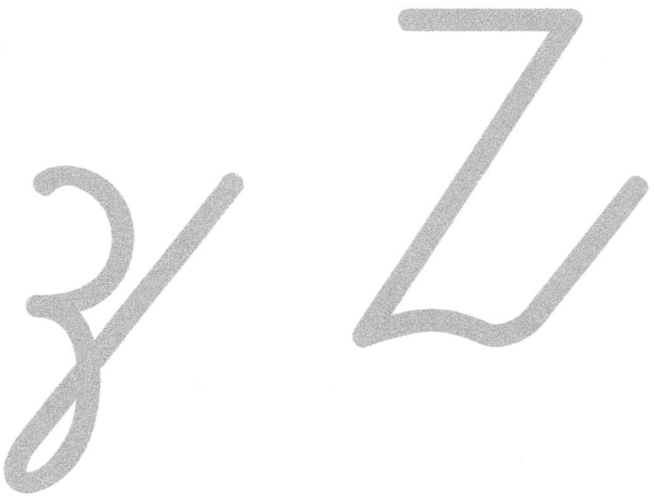

Proto-Semitic (ze)	Phoenician (zayin)	Etruscan (Z)	Greek (zeta)	Cyrillic (U)
=	I	I	Z ζ	З з

GER: 21 ENG: 26 Sum: 47

z Z

Zoo	Zone	Zahl	Zahn	Zeit
Zebra	Zinc	Zircon	Zenith	Zeppelin
Zambia	Zimbabwe	Zürich	Zuhai	Zambesi

a A

c C

d D

e E

f F

g G

h H

i I

j J

k K

l L

m M n N o O p P

q Q r R s S t T

u U v V w W x X

y Y z Z

Sütterlin (alte Schrift) - Old German Cursive Script